Dear Readers,

Names, dates, places, and incidents in this book have been changed or omitted for a variety of reasons, including but not limited to the security, safety, and wellbeing of the people, places or agencies involved. Any resemblance to anyone living or dead is purely co-incidental. I will leave it up to you the reader to realize what is what, who is who, and where is where.

Jodi Morley

Table of Contents

Chapter 1

IT happened. It wasn't supposed to happen but it happened all the same. It is always there. It haunts me daily. It influences every decision I make. And I don't know how to stop it.

Let me start at the beginning. I graduated from high school in 1995. I knew I was going to go to college but we didn't have a lot of money so I applied for student loans. I decided to take a few classes locally before transferring to my dream school: The University of Texas! I really don't know why I chose this school. I think it had something to do with the school colors (I know....real deep). I'd always liked earth tones and their burnt orange was beautiful. So I applied as a transfer student, ready to be a part of a school I had always looked up to. My plan was to study in the Pre-veterinarian coursework before transferring to Texas A&M, as they have a Veterinarian college. But that didn't happen. I never made it there. I never finished school at UT.

Everything was great at first. I moved up there with a great friend. We found a hip, new apartment complex that had its own bus to transport all us students to the UT campus a few miles away. I cannot tell you the amount of pride I felt stepping onto those grounds the first time. I was officially a Longhorn. What an amazing day. I took it all in. The Tower was beautiful. The buildings old and majestic. I was officially a Texas Longhorn! Hook 'Em!

Everything was normal. I attended class during the day time and worked at a restaurant in the evenings and at night to pay for rent and food. There was also time for fun. I went with my roommate down to 6th street for some rest and relaxation. For those that don't know it, it's basically a street full of bars and bars masquerading as restaurants.. I met a young man, whom was working at a local restaurant. He was kind, clean cut, and very friendly. We exchanged numbers and I was excited. I left the restaurant and ran into another young man, equally as charming AND he attended UT (Or so he said), lived in the apartment complex next to mine, and had an accent, which I found super sexy. He had a chiseled jaw-line and the kindest looking eyes. Plus he was funny. Things were looking up for me. I was ecstatic.

This one particular night, the first young man I had met called and said he wanted to come over. He did and we were watching television in my room. Things started happening and before I knew it, my panties were off. I was a virgin. I became frightened. I stiffened up. He told me "It's ok" and got up and dressed. But this story is not about him. He was a gentleman, even waiting to make sure I was ok before he left. This story is far more dark and painful.

This story is about the guy with the accent, which I no

longer find sexy. This is the story of a man that did whatever he wanted and changed my life forever. One moment in time..that's how the song goes, right? But oh that one moment was pure hell.

This one night after I got home from work, there was a huge party going on in the complex. And our particular apartment was right in the middle of it all. I could sit on my balcony and watch as people drank, danced, sang, and did whatever else inebriated people do.

Mr. Accent called and said he wanted to come see me. We had talked on the phone a few times and he seemed like a good guy, so I said sure. I took a quick shower, since I had just finished work. It was taking him a long time to come over, despite living right down the street. Finally, the phone rang. It was him at our gate. He sounded angry but I let him in anyways. I met him downstairs since the party was in full swing. I stood on the stairs waving him over.

He saw me and briskly walked over. He grabbed my arm and pulled me up three levels of stairs. Something was off. I didn't understand what was happening. I should have stopped right then and there to find out why he was so angry. But I didn't. Instead, I opened our apartment door and he barreled inside. I asked him what was wrong and he yelled at me that the line to get into the complex was too long and he was tired of waiting. I apologized saying I didn't know he had been waiting all that time but assured him I would finish getting ready and we would go downstairs to the party.

This is when it happened. I don't like to say the word. It's an ugly word. It's the word that has forever altered my life. Rape.

He grabbed me out of my bathroom where I was finishing my makeup, grabbing a fistful of hair as he threw me on the bed. I hit my head on the corner of the side table and became disoriented for a bit. I laid there feeling my head. There was a little gash bleeding on the side of my head in the hairline. I had a hard time really focusing on things at that time and kept having to close my eyes. That amount of time was enough for him to get my shorts and panties off. Enough time to penetrate me without my permission. Yeah...I said penetrate. Such an ugly word for such an ugly act. It was painful. I tried to fight him but he was too strong. Somehow, I really don't know how, but I managed to get my leg up and kick him. This resulted in him backhanding me across the face.

At this exact moment I thought I was dead. He pulled out a knife, like a hunting knife maybe? I really don't know, I just knew it was big. He told me "STOP!" as he held the knife to my throat. Now, I know that most rape advocate organizations recommend fighting but I stopped. I stopped fighting. There was so much noise from the party in the parking lot and none of my three roommates were home so I knew I couldn't find help. So I gave up. It haunts me to this day. I gave up, but it may have just saved my life.

He continued his thrusting but then decided that the missionary position just wasn't for him, or so I'm assuming because he yanked me off the bed and threw me down across my desk. Fuck that hurt but that was only the beginning. I could feel the knife against my back. I was just waiting for him to use it. But instead, he set it down on my back for a moment. I know this because I felt both his hands grab me and for lack of better wording, spread me open. Then there was so much pain. There was so much blood running down my leg. He had decided to be adventurous and try anal. I reacted like most people would, I think. I tightened up. It hurt so much that I had to get away. I could feel my skin tearing open. I felt him hit my back with the base of the knife. Again, he said one word, "STOP!". I tried but it hurt so much that I couldn't help tightening my muscles. I don't know how long this lasted, it felt like an eternity. He was aggressive, vicious. I'm pretty sure he was on some kind of drug. He enjoyed causing pain. He laughed at my pain. He pulled my hair, scratched my back, pinched whatever he could reach. When he finally finished, he grabbed me up by the hair and threw me back on the bed. I lay there crying, scared, bleeding, not knowing what was going to happen. He went to the bathroom to clean himself up.

So many things go through your mind at a time like that. All the horrible things he could do to you before he kills you. But also things and people you love. Would I live to see my parents again? Would they have to identify my body? What about the kids I always wanted to have? I'll never see my cat again. Would anyone even care? Then my mind switched to survival. Should I run out of the room? Should I run down to the party? Could I beat him out of my room and then out of the apartment?

I didn't have to decide what to do. He came back into the room. He looked at me and laughed. He laughed...again. I felt so humiliated. So small. Next he said, "Don't tell anyone about this or you're gonna meet my big knife again!" How fucking cute...like he's some big motherfucking mobster. I don't know, maybe he was in his country. Needless to say, I was scared. I realized all at the same time that I was going to live but I was going to have to remain silent. Writing that statement just now, "I realized I was going to live" seems so ridiculous now because the quality of that life changed so dramatically.

Last thing he said to me before walking out was "Change those fucking sheets. You got blood everywhere." More laughing followed. And then he was gone.

Chapter 2

And then he was gone. And yet he's never been gone. He lives in my head every day. He lives in my heart that is so afraid to let anyone in. He lives in my fears that I struggle with daily. He lives in my dreams. He lives in my desire for a future by constantly holding me down. He lives on in the lies I told about the rape. I attempted to tell a few people but instead made up a story where we had consensual sex. I just couldn't find a way to say the words. I was afraid but mostly, I was humiliated. But people needed some explanation as to why I had been acting strange so I made up the story. I told them we had consensual sex and I was just trying to reconcile how I felt about it. He lived on in all those lies for so many years. He lives on even now. But I don't.

For days following the rape, I stayed in my room. I called in sick to work, told my roommates to stay away. I withdrew from the world. I didn't know what to do. The bleeding had stopped, except when I used the restroom, it would start up again. My whole body ached. My anus hurt. I knew I probably needed to go to the doctor because I was pretty sure there was a tear. But then I'd have to explain. I could have lied but I didn't even think I could get a lie out without breaking down. So I stayed hidden and quiet until I realized that I had to go to school. I had to go to work.

So, finally, I decided to rejoin society. I got up, showered, cleaned my face, and practiced smiling. Yep. I had to practice smiling because it just didn't feel natural anymore. How do you go on after that? How do you talk to people after going through something like that?

I caught the bus and went to school. The University had always seemed big and domineering but now was just over-whelming. I suddenly couldn't remember where my classes were being held. I couldn't remember what class I had at what time. I looked it up and tried to find my way. People would talk to me and I would shy away from them. I couldn't make eye contact. Plus I had a slight bruise still on my cheek that I tried to cover with make-up. I'm sure I just seemed like an asshole, but I just wanted to be left alone. Alone was better. If your alone, you cant get hurt, right?

My grades suffered. Some days I went to class and others I stayed in my room and cried. I remember showing up to a Philosophy class only to find out it was test day and I hadn't read anything. I still got a D, which was a success for me at the time but only added to my feelings of inadequacy.

One night in particular, I sat at our dining room table at-tempting my Calculus homework. My best friend and roommate was helping me as she was a math major. I just couldn't get it. I didn't understand. It made no sense to me at all. I got so frustrated that I screamed something unintelligible and threw the book across the room. Then I collapsed in my friends arms and cried. She held me for a long while. We just sat there, not saying a word. Years later, I told her what had happened. She said she had always suspected. She even apologized for not doing more. It was not her fault. She did what I needed at the time. Besides, both of us were fighting our own demons.

We all decided that it might be a good time for a visit back home. My poor roommates came with me. I felt horrible because I just wanted to stay home wrapped in my mothers arms. I wanted to feel safe. So we didn't take them to Mexico, nor to South Padre Island, a beautiful beach nearly in our backyard. One passive aggressive roommate decided that she would send her family a post card about how horrible things were here. Of course, she left it in view of everyone. It made me feel even smaller. I had such good intentions to do things with them but instead, I didn't. I just wanted to be as close to my mother as possible.

My mom knew how lonely I had been so she took me to the Humane Society and adopted a cat. I named him Ranger and he was beautiful. He was gray with white circles around his eyes. He looked like a raccoon. Growing up my elementary school mascot was The Long Ranger, hence the name Ranger. But, it was not meant to be. Building inspectors came by the room about 5 weeks later. I was fined about 500 dollars and had to get Ranger out of the apartment asap. My parents took him back.

Exactly one week later, I was getting out of work and heard a faint crying. I knew it was a kitten. None of my coworkers would go look for the kitten with me. There was a train track that ran directly behind our restaurant and there was not much lighting. It was during the time of the Railway Murders (I think it was the serial killer Richard Ramirez) and people were scared. I decided I didn't care. I found this malnourished, scrawny little long haired black guy with the most beautiful yellow gold eyes. This cat, named Scurry, followed me everywhere. If I was having a bad day, there he was snuggling and purring. I still have that wonderful boy. 17 years old and still comforts mom to this day. Oh, and don't worry, we moved to an apartment that allowed me to keep him. And we've been together ever since.

Chapter 3

For those of you that have never experienced depression or anxiety before, let me try to explain. It's not your everyday, "I failed my math test, I'm so depressed" kind of affair. People try in their own way to encourage but usually end up making some asinine comment. I know what the books say about depression. Within a two week period, your mood should be depressed for most days of the week. There should be loss of interest in activities. Problems with weight, either gaining too much or losing too much. Poor sleep, which leads to fatigue. Speech and bodily movements are slowed. Self-esteem is gone, concentration is too difficult, and sometimes death seems like a viable solution. All of these criteria can be found in the DSM-V, which is basically the psychiatrists Bible.

But how does it really feel? There is this vast sense of emptiness that you can't fill. I would think that seeing my mother would fill that void but it didn't. I felt safer in her arms but that hole was still there. It felt like I was slowly being consumed by darkness. There is no light. There is no hope. Lethargy. I just didn't want to do anything. Going to the store was a chore. My arms felt heavy, like I could barely lift them. I was hungry all the time. I gained so much weight. I used food as a drug and still do. I wanted to sleep all day and night and took pills (Tylenol PM) to help with that. Problem was the Tylenol didn't stop the nightmares. I would wake up sweating and shaking, needing someone or something to hold. And that someone was usually Scurry. I'd go to the bathroom and vomit everywhere because I was so scared of my dreams. I would urinate in my bed at night when I had a particularly realistic nightmare. Now sometimes this depression lets you have a good day and you think things are going well and maybe, just maybe, you will be ok. But then BAM! Right back in your face, hurting more than ever.

I had flashbacks. I thought and felt like the rape was happening all over again. Sometimes my brain knew it wasn't happening, while, others I hid in the bathroom clinging to a kitchen knife. I started suffocating. I couldn't breath. I thought I was going to die as I was gasping for air. I don't know how long it took me to realize that I was breathing and just needed to find a way, any way, to calm myself down. And telling yourself "Calm Down" just doesn't work. I eventually started telling myself that I was safe. I was in a different apartment complex now and he didn't know where I was. I was safe. I was safe from this evil man but not from my own thoughts. My thoughts were dark and desperate. I couldn't handle it anymore.

Chapter 4

I decided I needed help. I went to the counseling center at UT. Problem was that I couldn't explain to the psychologist what was wrong. I would clam up. I would sit in silence and stare at the floor. The emotions inside of me were flowing. I was having what I would later discover to be a panic attack. Sadly, this happened every session. I eventually talked to her about my eating disorder. Yeah...that was a problem too but it wasn't THE problem at the time. After several sessions, the psychologist said my case was too difficult to be handled at the schools counseling center and I was referred out.

You can imagine how that felt. I finally came for help but got kicked out. Kicked out of counseling. I mean who gets kicked out of counseling? ME! That's pretty damn hard to do. And it wouldn't be the first time. There is only one counselor that has stood by me despite my difficulties and tendency to retreat when I get scared. One person that kept me even though I knew she was frustrated. One person that said she wasn't going anywhere. One person, besides family and friends whom did not give up on me. (This therapist, Dolores, came by much later, like 18 years or so later.)

So back to my many past adventures. I went to another counselor and again, focused on the eating disorder. She referred me to a nutritionist. Mackenzie. Mackenzie the dietician. She may have saved my life at that time. I never shared the rape with her. I almost did but I was afraid. Instead of sitting there, staring at me, she asked me questions. Just questions that brought me back to reality, that got me out of my head, that made me be present. We talked about the eating disorder too but she just knew how to get me to talk. She would remind me about my family and how much they loved me. She would talk to me about her family and their adventures. She was amazing.

However, no matter how great Mackenzie was, when I was alone, I couldn't escape my nightmare. I started having flashbacks of the rape and I didn't understand. I was so scared. I wanted it over so I decided to kill myself. All I had in my medicine cabinet was Tylenol and a full box of laxatives (which I used with my eating disorder). Needless to say, this did not end well. I'm sure you can imagine. I remember the moment that I passed out. I became so dizzy and fell over. I hit my hip on a vacuum cleaner that was in my room. Then there was nothing. I woke up with Scurry nudging me and meowing all while covered in vomit and ran (well more like crawled) to the toilet. I spent the next 5 hours vomiting and pooping all at the same time. But I survived. I felt like hell but I survived. And just for FYI, laxatives are never the way to go.

Another time I took an overdose of pills. My roommate found out and dragged me to the hospital. I still remember that emergency room. I didn't have a name. I was just the psych patient in room 5. The doctors came in and examined me. They asked what I had taken and I lied and told them more laxatives. When asked how many, I said, "Only about 15, I just wanted to get the food out of my body." None of that was true. I wanted to die. I had learned my lesson the first time with the laxatives so this time I took just the Tylenol. I really don't know how many, it was whatever was left in the bottle. If I had to guess, maybe 40 or so. The doctors in all their wisdom decided that I was not a danger to myself and sent me home. Granted, I cant really blame them since I lied the entire time.

I made it home just in time to vomit everywhere. My roommate tried to get me to lay down in her bed with her so she could make sure I was ok but I couldn't. I needed the toilet. I must have spent the entire night bowing to that toilet bowl. And spent the next few days with stomach pains.

These antics continued about 2 years. I really don't know how I survived. I didn't try very hard to survive. I missed out on so much during those years. I never went to a football game and anyone that knows me, knows I love my Horns. I never got to sing "The Eyes of Texas are Upon You". I never got to sing the Fight Song. I never got to see Bevo in person. It was like I was never a student. It was like I never existed.

I was running out of money because I missed work a lot. I

was doing poorly in all my classes and I didn't really come out of my room much. My parents called me home. They drove up to Austin and brought me back home, not knowing what was in store.

Chapter 5

It felt good to be home. It also felt like failure. I had failed in my dreams. I didn't graduate and I wasn't going to become a veterinarian. Hell, I didn't even know if I was going to live from day to day. I found a job at Video Stop, the video store I had worked at before moving. It was just what I needed. I loved that job and my coworkers. We had so much fun and slowly but surely that horrible memory started to disappear. As I would later learn, it didn't disappear, I just repressed it.

I remained depressed and anxious, I just didn't think much about the rape. However, I was very careful not to date. I couldn't do it. I still cant. That has always been a difficult subject to broach for me. People couldn't understand why I wouldn't date. I'd say, "Im just not interested or there's no good men down here." (I live at the tip of Texas so every-thing is "down here"). Funny story though. My grandmother, whom I love very much has a bit of a mouth. She doesn't care and will say whatever comes to her mind. One day over Christmas dinner, she asked me if I was a "lesbin". I looked at her and didn't know what the hell she was saying. I finally figured out she meant "lesbian". I told her no but to this day I think she believes I swing the other way. (and to give her credit, she was ok with it).

Now throughout this time, I saw countless numbers of therapists and psychiatrists. And I still couldn't bring myself to talk about the rape. I was placed on antidepressants. I still hurt inside and couldn't express myself. The memories were repressed but the emotions were not. I didn't know what to do but I quickly found that self-injury helped. And this was before self-injury was the "cool" thing to do. I hid my cuts well until one day I got so upset that I just sliced and sliced and sliced at my arm. It looked awful. Some cuts were pretty deep and took a long time to stop bleeding. No one knew what to do. Counsellors didn't help, doctors didn't help, nothing seemed to help. I felt like a lost cause.

I guess a year or so passed, I really don't remember. Things are still hazy. But my brother, who worked in the Financial Aid Department at our local University, decided it was time for me to return to school. He brought me a check one day and said, "Pick out your classes or you're going to owe a lot of money to the government!" So I picked my classes and returned to school. The University was about a 45 minute drive away so it was nice to be able to live at home. I was still having bouts of depression, anger, anxiety but I managed to perform well. I earned my Bachelors Degree in Psychology and followed that up with a Master's Degree in Clinical Psychology. If I couldn't help myself, maybe I could help someone else.

Chapter 6

After graduate school, I had a successful career. I was doing well, my clients were doing well. I was a successful therapist. I had friends at work that kept me entertained. They were so funny. I remember one day, the exterminator had been by in the morning. I had been at a meeting, so I returned to my office and there is a dead spider glued to my desk. I hate spiders. But they took the time to uncurl each spider leg to make it look alive and menacing. It was a brilliant prank... the jerks. But things looked like they were finally improving. I still took antidepressants but I was good for the first time in a long time.

I still wasn't dating. I hadn't dated since the rape. I couldn't do it. I also used food to provide me comfort, which helped make me less attractive to the opposite sex. But I desperately wanted a child. So I researched Artificial Insemination. And lo and behold, my obgyn did it. I went in, picked out my donor and waited until it was time. The only specifics I really requested in the donor was that he be at least 6 feet tall and have blue eyes. We tried the insemination 3 times and that third time was a charm. I was so happy. I remember thinking, "This is what happiness feels like". Pregnancy was normal...morning sickness, back pain, and pickles. Why pickles?.

My parents were on vacation visiting my aunt and uncle in Costa Rica when I found out the sex of the baby. I knew it was a boy. Had to be a boy. There are so many boys in our family. So the nurse asks if I'd like to know the gender. I said sure. It was a girl. A girl! I called my mom when I got home and told her it was a boy (she really wanted a girl). Then I broke the news and told her the truth. She started crying and was so excited.

Labor was induced on a Tuesday in October 2012 and my beautiful child was born on a Wednesday. I'm sure my mother remembers those two days very differently, because I can be a tad, tiny bit whiny, but I remember them as beautiful. I know there was pain but there was also this beautiful little being. When she was born, the doctor put her on my stomach. I'm not going to lie, I panicked. What am I supposed to do with it? Oh my God! This is mine! Mind you, I still hadn't touched her yet. So I gently touched her with just a few fingers until she was whisked away for examination.

I had never been so happy in my life.

But I didn't know what was to come.

Chapter 7

What was to come was pure hell. It was hospitalization, medications, therapy, and that's just the medical part. Soon after I came home with my most precious gift, my daughter Callie, I also came back with something more sinister. I started off just feeling depressed. Ok..so that's normal for new mothers. I continued to work but started to feel paranoid. I had worked in a city about 30 minutes away (I'm a Texan, we go by minutes not miles). But I started to feel like I needed to be closer to my daughter. My childhood friend was caring for her during the day and I knew how good she was to Callie. But I wanted to be closer so I transferred to my city but stayed within the same company. That was better, right? Nope. I lost all my supports. All the people I cared most about were gone. I couldn't just walk around the corner and say hey. This new work environment was brutal. There were some girls there that we called "The Mean Girls". They were very much like Regina George and her gang. During one of the hiatuses that I had from work (I'll get into that more later), the gang leader actually said she was glad I was sick and hoped I never returned. Wow. What a horrible person. So I was basically by myself with a couple of close friends. These friends are still close to this day and I love them dearly.

I started having flashbacks again. Except these were far worse. I had tactile hallucinations with them. So not only did I feel the fear and see the images and hear his words, but I could also feel him touching me. Yes. I could actually feel him touching me, penetrating me. I can only imagine what I looked like. I can't say for sure. I would become hysterical crying and I remember hiding in the corner of the room or the bathtub trying to stop whatever was happening.

Now I am a trained therapist. I knew what was happening. But I couldn't stop it. It felt so real that at times I actually believed he was going to walk in that door again. I would cry and scream and yell at myself that it wasn't real but nothing worked. I would hit myself in the head shouting that it wasn't real. I could feel myself losing the battle. I started cutting myself again. It's weird, I know, but cutting allowed me to focus on the blood and the pain and not the hallucinations. It made me feel something real, something tangible. I liked seeing the blood. It felt like I was releasing the evil. But the evil got deeper and deeper, which meant I had to cut deeper and deeper. Too deep. I would sit in the bathroom praying for the bleeding to stop. Then sometimes I would poke at the wound trying to keep it bleeding so I could bleed out.

I knew I needed help but didn't know how to get it. I still hadn't told anyone about the rape. I couldn't handle it anymore so I texted my best friend Kathleen. I told her what was happening. She convinced me to tell my mom. So I did.

Things didn't get easier after telling my parents. I became more embarrassed about my symptoms. It had been about 15 years since it happened and there it was, right in my face as if it happened yesterday.

I took more FMLA from work. There was no way I could be there. I couldn't even handle my own problems, how could I handle someone else's?

Chapter 8

Now you'll have to forgive me. My memory of the next few years is shaky at best. What I do know is that I was hospitalized on an in-patient psychiatric ward. I would be hospitalized a total of nine times to date. Now for those that have never had the pleasure, it's such a great experience. You start out being frisked and having your hair checked for contraband. Then you go into an Intake room where you are asked a bunch of questions. That's fun but it gets even better! After you are officially admitted, they take all your belongings. They put you in a room and make you strip and put on a hospital gown, which is difficult when you are a big girl. It's so hard to cover all the necessary parts. The nurse comes in and makes notes of all the marks on your body. Then my favorite part: you have to squat with no panties and cough. They make you do this several times. The nurse explained that people like to hide things (pills, razors) inside their vagina or anal cavity. This is kind of what I figured but it still felt so inhumane. Humiliated. Scared.

I get it. I understand why it has to be done. It's just overwhelming to a rape victim experiencing hallucinations. But I kept it together. I put my clothes back on and was led out into the living room area. It's an odd feeling, people checking you out. It's a lot like prison I would assume (or at least from what I've learned from Orange Is The New Black). But then something happens, patients start walking up and introducing themselves. It feels a bit like Misfit Island. There's people from all walks of life. There are gang members, criminals, truck drivers, professionals, teachers. I met so many different people and we all had one thing in common. We needed help. No one was better than anyone else and if you're having a bad day, someone would try and cheer you up.

I can remember during one hospital stay, there was a young man with multiple problems and he was clearly in need of special education treatment. He would get so upset and start hitting himself in the head. The other patients seemed to take turns caring for him. During one episode, a new patient became violent (it happens as it is a psychiatric unit), and about 6-7 patients started yelling, "Get Gary!" They wanted to make sure he was away from the violence. They were so caring. It was amazing to see.

I found myself wanting to help others too but I had too many problems with myself. So mostly I sat there trying to contain my own psychological monsters.

Chapter 9

Dr. Almeda. How can I explain Dr. Almeda? When I first started having problems after I had my daughter, I thought, she would be perfect to see. She's a woman and a mother, maybe she would be more understanding. And at first she was but as our sessions grew on, she became more and more irritated with me. And she doesn't hide emotions well. She told me that being in the mental health industry myself, I should know and do more to improve my health. She said I needed to start exercising ok, ok…fair assessment. But what she couldn't understand was why I wasn't improving. In fact, I kept getting worse. So of course, that was my fault. I must not be taking the medications correctly or at all. I must be using other substances along with my medications that were causing a bad interaction and increased depression and anxiety. She would suggest things like going to the park or volunteering at a nursing home. All nice things, which would be great, if I hadn't just told her that my panic attacks have become so common that I cannot leave the home. If I do leave my house, my mother has to be with me.

She continued to have selective hearing in what I was saying.

Her best advise for cutting was to just stop. She told me that as a therapist myself, I knew what to do. And she was right. I know what you are supposed to do but actually doing them was so hard. I tried the ice on the skin, the rubber band method, drawing on one's skin to ease that temptation to cut. Nope, it didn't work. These ideas must have been made up by people that have no idea how it feels to have a mental illness. I regret ever suggesting them in therapy sessions with my clients. Nothing feels as satisfying as watching your own blood run down your arm.

She would often fuss at me that I was not doing my part. She was doing everything she could, my therapist Dolores, was doing everything she could, and then there was me. I refused to walk. Yep. That's the horrible thing that I didn't do and I was belittled because of it. Meanwhile, I'm sitting over here thinking, "Yay, I showered AND shaved my legs!" I think she overestimated my abilities. But things were always about weight, which I understand is healthy for the entire body, including the brain. One day, I remember her saying that it was not possible for me to continue to feel so depressed with all the medications I was taking. It was around the 6 pill mark, daily. Some pills I took three times a day for my anxiety. Another session, she told me she was going to have to discontinue our services if I continued to present as suicidal. So those were lovely mixed messages. Do I tell the truth and get kicked out of services. If I do I tell the truth, will I get some help? Or do I just remain silent because the people that are supposed to help me can't help me when

I'm considering taking my own life.

One positive thing to come out of my visits with her was that she asked for a DNA test. A DNA test to see which medications my body reacted with best. Initially she said that she didn't have the test yet and wanted me to go through a certain company that she was waiting on. My mother decided to research, as mothers do, and found a facility in Houston that would carry out that testing. I quickly told Dr. Almeda about it and she said no because she wanted it from a certain University. So we didn't do it. We should have done it but the doctor had said no so we waited. Doctors know best, right? About 6 months down the road, she received the testing products and I did my little mouth swab and sent them off to be tested.

Finally vindication! Yep, you read that right! Vindication. I continuously told her I didn't feel good and she continuously told me, in not so many words, that it was my fault. "The medications can only do so much Jodi. The rest must come from within." Guess what? Every single medication she had me on besides clonazepam was not a good match for my DNA. We changed to those that were listed as positive interactions and it was amazing. It was like the fog lifted a little. I could endure more. My PTSD symptoms lessened. I still had problems, mind you, but I was on my way to better days,

And then this happened.

I had stopped seeing her in April 2016 because my insurance (thanks Obamacare) changed from a PPO to an HMO. She didn't accept HMO insurance and I would be stuck paying 200 or so dollars for a few minutes of her time. I explained this to the receptionist and I cancelled my appointment. The receptionist understood and said she would keep my file open just in case I needed to come back. I explained that my Primary Care Physician had agreed to prescribe the medications for me.

Well for these last few months, my health has really been failing and I haven't been able to see my PCP to discuss possible changes in medications. Its getting closer to the time of the year when the rape happened. I usually do poorly around this time. So my mom said she would pay for the appointment. I called. The receptionist set me up for an appointment that week. Except, she called me back saying that Dr. Almeda was refusing to see me because I had not been compliant. I reminded her secretary about our discussion and explained that I remained compliant with everything. Nothing had changed. I told her, "Well that's fine if she doesn't want to see me. I guess I'll find some other way". The secretary called me back once more and said Dr. Almeda had experienced a change of heart and was agreeing to see me. Mini victory I thought.

I got to her office on time and waited. I had brought my mother with me as I needed help explaining how difficult things have been lately. She called me in but only wanted to see me. She didn't want my mother in the room. First thing out of her mouth, and no this is not a joke, was "Well I can tell you're still not exercising". Self-esteem knocked down a rung. Then she wants to know why I have chosen to come back and what I needed her for. I explained that my symptoms were becoming more difficult to deal with. I wasn't having flashbacks, per say, or at least not the ones I used to have. It was more like intrusions. Seeing images, pictures of what this man was doing to me. I was having panic attacks again and had to hide out in the bathroom for a 15 or more minutes while at a child's party, until I was finally able to calm down (which is a huge deal in my eyes…I stayed at the party instead of running away.) Then she became irritated because I had forgotten my medication bottles and now she had to contact my PCP to identify the medications were truly what I said they were.

I had told her that I stopped the clonazapam on my own because I didn't want to get addicted but I felt like I needed it again, You could see on her face that she was irritated with me for bringing this up and suggesting how to do her job. I was just reminding her what had helped me in the past. Next she asked me if I was working yet. I explained that I was not and she rolled her eyes, as if disgusted by my neediness. "Are you still on disability? When does that end?" I explained that I was still receiving disability because I still could not return to my work. I can't be a therapist right now but I also can't work at a store or restaurant because of my anxiety. Again she rolled her eyes.

One of the last things she asked me was if I was still seeing Dolores, my therapist. I told her yes and she wondered out loud why I would still be doing that because clearly she wasn't helping me much. This really upset me and I wanted to yell at her, "Dolores is the ONLY one that helps me!" But I didn't because I have no backbone.

So she prescribed some medications and then told me that I needed to find another psychiatrist that is in network instead of seeing her. So as a depressed person with anxiety and PTSD, this did not go over well. But maybe it's for the best. What is it that hip people say these days? "Bye Felicia!"

Chapter 10

The Hospitalizations. My first hospitalization occurred between 3/8/2013 and 3/15/2013. I had been having a very difficult time at work. I was crying non-stop, having trouble focusing, and desperately wanted to die. It was a few days after my birthday and I felt like a complete failure. I didn't feel worthy of living this life anymore. I was damaged. I'm still damaged. My daughter was a few months old at this time. It was tough being a mom, being severely depressed, having panic attacks, and having Post Traumatic Stress Disorder. I loved that little girl so much but I just didn't feel like I could go on. I didn't deserve her. She was so wonderful and I was a horrible mother. The best thing I could do for my child was to leave her in the loving arms of her grandparents. That's what depression said anyways.

I was having tactile hallucinations at this time as well. This left me in an always anxious state that I could never escape. Not even during sleep. I would still wake up and feel him. It was awful. I was telling my best friend, Kathleen, about my problems. I told her I loved her and thanked her for always being there for me. That, of course, made her suspicious. She, being in the mental health field as well, talked to me and was able to get me to admit my plans. I was going home to take my medications. An overdose. I would make sure my daughter was cared for and at my parents home and I would overdose. Well, Kathleen wasn't having any of that. She got with another friend, Benjamin, who happened to be in charge of the Crisis Department at our place of work. He called Doctor's Hospital (DHR) and secured a bed for me. They didn't ask me. They just did it because that's what friends are for. They drove me to the hospital. I can't say I was too happy with them at the time but I would have done the same for them.

I called my parents to tell them I was on the way to the hospital. My parents were worried obviously but knew it needed to be done. After Intake was completed, the nurse checked my body for marks. They found bruising all over my thighs. I had been hitting my legs with a hammer whenever I felt the tactile hallucinations. I guess I felt like I was beating him away each time I smashed my leg. It hurt like hell but was oddly satisfying.

I stayed in the hospital for eight days. I honestly don't re-member much from those days. I was out of commission. I shut down. I didn't participate. I didn't really talk to anyone, although most tried to communicate with me. I just felt so far gone to even try anymore. I was placed on differ-ent medications. I was prescribed Klonopin, Risperdal, and Effexor. The Klonopin was helpful. It helped to calm my anx-iety. I still had the flashbacks, depression, hallucinations but I was a little more calm.

While I was in the hospital, my tactile hallucinations were becoming worse and more frequent. I had taken to going into the restroom and hitting my arm with my fist. I would also slam my arm against the sink. Whatever I could do to cause pain. At home, I would do the same thing except I would use a hammer to bang my arms and legs. My brain could interpret physical pain but it didn't know what to do with the hallucinations.

While in the hospital during this stay, I hit myself so much that my arm was completely bruised and swollen. They were afraid it might be broken but it wasn't. So I was put on a one-to-one, meaning someone followed me everywhere. I could go to the restroom by myself but my guard would stand outside banging on the door if I took too long. They went with me to lunch. They sat with me in the living quarters. They sat in a chair next to my bed as I slept. But they also shared all the good stuff with me. They told me about using the restroom in the hallway to shower because it had warm water, while our rooms were freezing cold. I was given first choice of snacks and an extra drink when needed. Silly I know, but such good information to have when your on the "inside".

The day I was released was scary. I had been literally locked in a room with nurses and rehabilitation technicians. I was made to get up in the morning. I was told where to go for exercise. I was told when to eat and what to eat. I didn't know if I could make all those decisions on my own.

But I was released anyway. It's odd but there is a bit of a honeymoon period where you think, "I can do this! I will survive." And then after a day or so, reality sinks in. And sometimes reality sucks. I still had this precious little angel at home to take care of. I felt inadequate. I had to return to work. I had to make money so I could pay my mortgage. I had to live. But could I?

Chapter 11

The second hospitalization was much like the first, except this time I was referred by my psychiatrist. And I use the term referred very loosely, as she had told me she would call the police if I didn't show up at DHR. I was there from 3/18/2013-3/22/2013. Five more days in this God awful hospital. Looking back on it though, the hospital was great. The staff were well trained and helpful when needed. I just didn't want to be there. They were preventing me from doing what I wanted to do: DIE. Again, I was discharged with a medication change and referred back to my psychiatrist.

I returned once again to the hospital in April 2013. I stayed at DHR from 4/19/2013-4/24/2013. I was quickly learning the ropes of this hospital, not a good sign. I had been cutting again and had a very large gash on my leg. I had it covered with steri-strips but it was still bleeding. The nurses added some bandages and it was agreed that stitches were not needed, or at least not yet. I hated the hospital. It was cold, so, so very cold. There would be outside breaks, which consisted of a small yard with a mega high concrete wall. You couldn't see out and no one could see in. I loved these breaks because I had the chance to go warm up in the sun.

Only problem is that "Outside Break" was really just code for "Smoking Break". I have asthma so I couldn't go out when they were smoking. I had to beg the technicians to take me outside. Most were unsympathetic, saying everyone got treated to the same breaks. Even the nurses seemed to have little care for my plight. However, I can be quite persistent and I finally started getting some outside time. And it wasn't just me. The other patients, even those that smoked, rallied behind me to encourage an outside break with no smoking (as long as they still had their break of course).

I managed to stay out of the hospital for a few months. I continued to work. But in August I relapsed. Now, I use the term "relapse" rather loosely. I had continued to have problems but had somehow managed to remain at my job and in my own home. But in early August 2013, I started to take Tylenol. Large amounts of Tylenol. Everyday. I was trying to hurt myself. The Tylenol made me feel horrible, which is how I thought I should feel for being the horrible, damaged person that I now was. I had an appointment with Dr. Alameda. I told her what I had been doing and guess where I ended up yet again? DHR. They ran lab work and surprisingly everything looked ok. On a side note, Dr. Alameda made me feel like such a loser once again. She told me, "Jodi, you are smarter than that. You know you need to take more Tylenol to kill yourself." So I can't even kill myself adequately. I went through boxes and boxes of Tylenol. But I would always end up vomiting. These were almost violent vomiting sessions. My whole body would shake. My stomach would burn. Had my body not rejected the medication, I'm certain I would have died.

Dr. Alameda's secretary also called me while I was on the road to the hospital with my mom. She told me that she had failed to collect my co-pay and would like to do it on the phone. My brain was saying "What the fuck??" But my mouth said, "Umm…ok." We had, I'll use the word "discussed", going to the hospital. I was very much against it but the doctor, for valid reasons, believed I needed to be in-patient. So when the secretary called to collect my co-pay I was so pissed. Really? You can't wait until next time I see you to charge me? I gave her the information and then hung up on her. But I certainly didn't get the same kind of satisfaction hanging up on my IPhone as I would have a landline. Remember those? Man, you could have great arguments with those.

I stayed in the hospital for 3 days this time. I had figured them out. I knew what to say to get out. "I feel like the new medication has improved my mood significantly and I no longer feel the need to kill myself." Great news to hear. You are ready to be discharged. I know, I was only hurting myself and my family. I know that now but I just didn't feel any use for the hospital. It's only purpose was to keep me safe. Ok.. so that's a big deal. But nothing ever helped me to deal with the reasons for the suicidal ideations. I would see a therapist but we never talked much. She always said that there wasn't enough time to work on my issues in only a few days and she would let my therapist handle that. Mostly, we sat around a room with a television watching horrible movies and waiting. Waiting for morning medications. Waiting for breakfast. Waiting for smoke break. Waiting for gym time (which was my favorite because they had a basketball hoop. I'd go off by myself and shoot the ball, repeatedly until it was time to go.) Then we would wait for another smoke break, followed by waiting for lunch. Then we would wait for Occupational Therapy, Group Therapy, Visitation, night-time medications, and then bed time.

Bed time was awful. That's when the demons attacked. They were present through the day but they were especially present at night. Night time was the hardest. But I had to pretend to be ok as the technicians made their nightly rounds. Sometimes I would hide in the bathroom and hit my legs to feel something other than the hallucination.

Then in November 2013, I was corresponding with a counselor from my insurance company. My insurance had a neat service that allowed you to have a counselor to email or talk to on the phone when needed. We were having a discussion and I mentioned to her that I was having intense suicidal thoughts again. I wrote something vague, something that could lead the counselor to believe I was going to kill myself. My message to her had been so short as I was presenting at a training on none other than Suicide. Yeah..I see the irony there too. So I had sent that last message and wasn't able to check again for another hour or so. The last message the counselor had left me was that she was going to call my towns Crisis Center because she really was fearful that I was going to take my own life. And here's a fun tidbit, I actually worked for the Community Health Center that responded to the "Crisis". So I got called out of the training to talk to a Crisis worker. He asked me many questions about my history and I was honest with him. Now I was feeling suicidal, which is a daily occurrence but I wasn't actively trying to kill myself. But because of my history, he decided it was best for me to be admitted. Not only admitted but Sectioned 26. A Section occurs when the person does not want to go to the hospital but clearly needs to or for when they are being combative. A judge signs the order and has a police officer pick the patient up and escort them to the psychiatric hospital. I still don't see the need to have sectioned me but I was picked up right then and there by an officer that seemed less than thrilled to do her job. So, technically, I'm a badass, since I've ridden in the back seat of a police car, which isn't very comfortable. Needless to say, I spoke to the psychiatrist the next day and told him what happened. He agreed to discharge me.

One of the worst hospitalizations occurred on or around 12/21/2013. I had gone to see my PCP because I had cut myself too deep and it wouldn't stop bleeding. She decided she wanted me sent to the hospital. My normal hospital was at capacity so I couldn't stay there. But they found a bed for me at another hospital, so we went home got my clothes I would need and left. I had been cutting my thigh, trying to hide the marks from my family and friends. I knew that I probably needed stitches but wasn't going to tell anyone. So we get to the hospital and I tell the receptionist that Dr. Esparza had referred me there. She proceeds to call the Adult Unit to see if there was a Dr. Esparza there. (You would think she would know what doctors are working in her facility). I was trying to keep quiet about it because some friends from work were there admitting a client into the hospital. At about this time, I look down and my jeans are saturated with blood. I ran into the restroom and pulled down my jeans. The blood was gushing out of my leg for some reason. My mom went to get me a pair of shorts to change into while staff at the hospital sprang into action. They had called 911 because they couldn't get enough pressure on the leg to stop the bleeding. My mom came back and I changed and then waited for the paramedics. They arrived and took me to the medical hospital. Again I was referred to as the psych patient. The attending doctor lectured me on the cutting and stitched me up and I was ready to go back to the psychiatric unit. This is a much older hospital than the one I usually frequented but, honestly, I liked it better. I had my own room, so I didn't have to share the restroom with anyone. The hot water worked (a little too well as I nearly burned myself). The staff was very nice. The psychiatrist that attended to me when my leg was bleeding even came over during breakfast to ask how I was feeling. She wasn't even my assigned psychiatrist. So all in all, this was a successful hospitalization. I don't remember feeling frustrated or scared. It was a relaxed environment.

Then from 6/24/2014 through 6/27/2014 I was hospitalized once again at DHR. Dr. Alameda had seen me for a follow-up in her office and decided it would be best for me to go inpatient. My thoughts of suicide were becoming worse. I was taking copious amounts of Tylenol at work. I had the attitude of "whatever happens, happens." I was a model patient. I always did what the staff had asked of me and never mouthed off. But this was just part of my plan to get out sooner. Behave, act like nothing is wrong and tell the psychiatrist how you have "seen the light" and are no longer suicidal. It was a Christmas miracle in June. Needless to say, Dr. Alameda caught on and lectured me about my poor behavior and inability to accept help when I needed it.

The last hospitalization that I remember occurred in April. 4/6/2015-4/9/2015 to be exact. I had become increasingly out of control. I was taking more and more pills, never anything illegal, just whatever I could find at the pharmacy. I was buying bottles and bottles of Tylenol. I was so tired by this point, I could hardly do my job. I had increasing sadness, more nightmares, hopelessness, poor concentration and the list goes on. I would have flashbacks in the middle of a therapy session. I would have to tell them that I had an emergency so I needed to leave or I would text my boss from the bathroom explaining why I couldn't keep going and that I needed help excusing the client out of my office. That was hard. I loved my clients and they needed me but I was fighting my own demons. It was after this hospitalization that I decided to quit my job. I simply could not put another persons life in jeopardy. In a way, this was the best decision and the worst decision. But in the end, I had to do the right thing.

So I gave my two weeks notice. I was going to quit the job I had for about 9 years. But it had to be done. The majority of cases were individuals that had been sexually assaulted and so there were a lot of triggers. I worked with children and adolescents and this made it so hard to say good bye. For many of them, I was the only person they could talk to.

I ended up quitting that week instead of waiting my two weeks. My flashbacks were still horrible and easily set off. I would often start crying in my office for no known reason. The last straw, however, came when my direct supervisor told me I would have to speak to this one family because their daughter had just been raped. I really enjoyed talking to this young woman but I knew I couldn't help her at that time. I knew it would induce a flashback and I just couldn't see putting her through that. So my supervisor told the family I would be unable to meet with them and they became angry. They wanted to know why they could see me before (someone had already given them an appointment with me.) My supervisor sided with the family and let the appointment remain. Then my supervisor told me that our clients have rights and we must abide by them. I became so angry with her that she wasn't taking my own health into consideration. So I quit a week earlier. I called our Human Resources Department and explained that I could not honor my 2 weeks notice. I apologized profusely and the upper management was understanding. The allowed me to leave that Friday. I was still going to be forced to see the rape victim but on that day, I called in sick to work. I had actually come down with a stomach virus. I'm sure they think I was lying but I can assure it was not a lie. It was a horrible, horrible virus.

Chapter 12

We were desperate for anything to work. My mother kept saying, "I'm going to lose you". Man, I put her through hell. She needed, wanted anything to work so the doctor suggested Electroconvulsive Therapy. The closest place that did this was a Mental Health Hospital in San Antonio. So we packed up the baby and went in for a consultation. I say that like "yeah..we just got in the car and boom we were there". Not exactly. It takes a good 4 hours to get to San Antonio. We found a La Quinta that was down the street from the hospital. This La Quinta would become like family to us. The staff all knew us and we were treated extra special. I even got the nicest card from the woman in charge of the free breakfast.

So we decided to talk to the psychiatrist at this hospital about ECT. We made our appointment, discussed the process and decided to give it a try. So what they do is hook up electrodes to your head and shock you causing a seizure which stimulates those parts of the brain that cause depression. Or at least that's my understanding of it. We would stay in San Antonio about a month and have sessions every other day. Then afterwards, we would drive back to San

Antonio each week and have a session each Monday.

The room they would do the ECT in was about the size of a small bedroom. There was a restroom in one corner. The rest of the room was divided by curtains to create these little makeshift rooms. Each little room had a bed and oxygen tank. The room was small but the staff was fast and effective. When a bed opened up, meaning someone's treatment was over and they had been sent home, they promptly took you inside. They asked you to use the restroom first and then return to bed. Shoes were removed and an IV was started. Next a nurse put electrodes all over your scalp. Then you would wait for your turn. The machine that sent the current through the electrodes was wheeled from room to room.

An Anesthesiologist would come by right before the psychiatrist came in. He/She would ask questions: Are you allergic to anything? Have you eaten anything passed 10:00 pm last night? Have you taken your medications this morning? Have you ever had any trouble with anesthesia before? All these questions just added to my already high anxiety. Next the doctor would come in. The nurse would give you a foam bite block to prevent you from accidentally biting your tongue off. Sound fun yet? Next they would put an oxygen mask on you over the bite block. I've always hated oxygen masks because I feel like I'm suffocating. Everyone tells me that is irrational because it's pure oxygen but it sends my anxiety skyrocketing. Next the doctor injects a muscle immobilizer (not sure the real term) and then injects the medication to put you to sleep.

Most times things ran smoothly but there was one time that still gives me nightmares. Everything had gone as planned until the muscle immobilizer was given. Next I was given the medication to put me to sleep but it was not enough. It was such a horrible experience not being able to move. I couldn't breathe. I could hear the doctors conversing, saying I was still awake and wondering if the medication had been miscalculated, had I gained weight? But thankfully I was given more medication and I knocked out. The anesthesiologist later told me that I was breathing because she was breathing for me. Well, she needed to pump that thing faster because I can tell you I was suffocating! After you fall asleep, they turn on the machine and send the electrical currents throughout your brain. Then they unhook everything and let you sleep for about 30 minutes. Next, they wake you up and walk you out to the car to make sure you get there safely. Someone has to pick you up as you cannot drive.

During one session, there were some nursing students observing the ECT that morning. I had the psychiatrist step into my room and ask me if I would be willing to speak to these students about my experiences. He said, "I think you have the intelligence to help them understand what its like to go through the process." Now I was flattered but did not feel intelligent enough to elegantly explain the experience. What he didn't know is that I was having a particularly difficult day and really wasn't in the mood to talk to strangers or anyone for that matter. Also, my anxiety was especially high that day which makes it more difficult to function. It feels like my brain is on high alert. So these poor nursing students didn't get much from me. I felt like a politician, saying the same thing repeatedly but essentially saying nothing. I felt like an idiot. Maybe even a caveman, just a grunt here and there.

All in all, I had 22 sessions and overall, it wasn't a bad experience. My mom felt like it helped me some. She could tell a slight difference in my mood. It definitely didn't change it as much as I would have liked. Plus, I later discovered memory loss. The doctors had told me that memory loss was a possibility but it shouldn't be too bad. Well, they were wrong. Not only can't I remember things that happened in my month long "vacation" in San Antonio but I also have trouble remembering things that happened when I was younger. My mom tells me stories of us traveling around San Antonio. We went to the River Walk, rode in one of the boats down there. We ate at the Rainforest Café, which apparently Callie loved. We went to Six Flags Amusement Park and played on the huge carousel. We rode a trolley because at this time she loved Daniel Tiger and there was a trolley in the show. We passed by this restaurant called "The Magic Mushroom" and I would tell my mom we needed to try it out because it seemed interesting. God Bless my mom. She would just tell me that we ate there a few days ago and I had liked a different pizza joint much better. Lol. I wish I could say I have these memories but I don't.

It also haunts my memories from the past. I have trouble remembering friends names. I usually recognize faces but then I'm not sure if I know them from high school, college, or work. And I definitely can't remember their names, It makes me feel horrible because all these people were important to me at some point in my life and yet, I can't remember them. Friends will say, "Remember when we did this or that? It was so funny!" But I don't remember. My mom will talk about pets we had growing up and I might remember what they looked like but not their names. Hell, I can't remember some of the names of the pets we have right now.

And I feel like my mind functions much slower. I used to be really quick with a joke but now I'm the last one to the party. Puzzles are harder to complete. Books are harder to read because I don't always know what the words mean. I used to enjoy reading but now it just makes me feel stupid. I feel like half the person I was before. I'm embarrassed to go out to eat or just hang out with old friends because there is a significant difference in my abilities. I've considered going back to school but I'm not sure I could keep up.

CHAPTER 13

Nothing seemed to be working. I had more hospitalizations after the ECT and still kept experiencing my symptoms. I was getting frustrated that nothing was working. A new treatment became available at DHR called Transcranial Magnetic Stimulation or TMS. I spoke with the person in charge of the treatment and I was invited in for a consultation. They thought I would be a good candidate and I started the treatment. Now that was a unique experience. They start out placing electrodes on certain places on your head. Then they turn on the machine and see what part of your body wiggles. It was pretty funny and felt completely strange. They narrowed down the placement of the electrodes by trial by error. Basically, they had to hit a certain part of the brain for the TMS to work efficiently and a certain part of your body moved when they had the correct spot.

Now the doctor and caseworker had both assured me that it didn't hurt. It may be uncomfortable but it shouldn't hurt. Well, they were wrong. When the machine starts there is a loud banging noise that coincides with the loud banging in my head. They give you ear plugs as to not damage your hearing. During the first treatment the doctor, who is a psychiatrist, asked me what it felt like. I told him it felt like a nail was being hammered into my head. He laughed and said he had never heard that description before. He said most people have a slight headache and feel a pulsing as the machine does its work. They decreased the intensity of the pulsation and it was a little better. I had to drive to Edinburg for the treatment three times a week. I didn't mind. These were good people and they really seemed to care about my welfare (the psychiatrist and the caseworker were both excellent). In fact, I tried to change psychiatrists and see him instead but he didn't accept my insurance. Which was a bummer because he was so kind and caring.

Did it work? Well, I completed the Beck Depression Scale II once a week during the treatment and my numbers did go down, showing less depressive symptoms. I guess I could feel a little difference but it just wasn't enough. I started cutting again as a coping skill. Needless to say my treatment ended and I was once again left to my own devices.

Chapter 14

As of this writing, I'm still struggling. People are tired. I am tired. It is so hard to get up and out of bed. I do get up because I have a little girl watching me. My daughter is the most precious child and I love her so much. She is so intuitive. She knows when I'm having a bad day. She's only three, mind you, but she understands. She's grown up with mommy going into and out of hospitals her whole life. During those hospital stays, I wasn't allowed to see her because children under a certain age are not allowed during visitation hours. She is the reason I always wanted out of the hospital so badly, because I wanted my child, my reason for trying to live.

She will ask me on certain days, "Mommy, do you feel bad?" How do you answer that to a three year old? Yes mommy is feeling sick. She always has some kind of child-like advice: "Take some medication so you can get better." She will ask my mom if mommy is getting sick again. Or sometimes she will tell me to go lay down in bed. When I do go to the room to lay down, she will often come with me. She brings her computer tablet and her puppy and sits in the bed next to me. Sometimes she will rub my back but she always tells me she loves me. This is why I fight. I want to give up. I am tired. But I love that little girl. A little girl I always wanted. A little girl I never thought would be possible after that fateful night in October. I am fighting for her and she deserves to have her mother, a healthy mother.

Chapter 15

After visiting my psychiatrist and being told that she would only continue to see me until I found another provider, I decided to keep my appointment with my Primary Care Physician. She had been dispensing the medication for me since I couldn't afford the appointments with Dr. Alameda. I was hopeful that I would get some kind of help from her. My appointment was at 2:30 and I was called back at 3:00. My doctor came in. She was her normally cheerful self. She asked how I was doing and I explained that I was struggling again (still). The next thing she told me took me by surprise. She said I have demons in me that are keeping me from healing. She explained that when a traumatic event occurs, the demons have an easy opening to grasp hold of us. She said the demons had their talons in me and were not letting go.

She prayed for me. And then asked, "Jesus, what is the lie?" I didn't know what to say so I just sat there. She asked me if I had accepted Jesus into my heart and I said I didn't know. So she had me repeat several statements asking and allowing Jesus into my heart. Then she started asking again what the lie was. I told her the first thing that popped in my head, whether it be divine intervention or not. I said, "I am ruined, damaged." She then said, "And what is the truth? What does Jesus say is the truth?" I replied the opposite, that I was not damaged.

Now at this point I start to feel overwhelmed with emotion. I started to realize that I wasn't going to get any help in the form of a medication change. And I began to cry. And sure enough, she told me that changing the medications were not going to do anything for me because it was really the demons that were attacking me. She explained that the demons were very strong and I would likely need more than one person to pray for me. She began to pray over me and even spoke in tongues. She told me several times that she just wanted me to feel better, which I believe. However, I left there feeling lost. I left there feeling like there is no hope for me. Do I even believe in demons? I guess I do but that wouldn't be my medical diagnosis. I didn't understand what I'm supposed to do with this information.

I've had people tell me that before, that I have demons and need to rid myself of them by having people lay hands on me. As a rape survivor, it is very hard to have people touching me. My doctor, while she was praying for me was holding my hand and rubbing my back. I felt comforted by this as I know her, yet there was still a part of me that was screaming to run, to hide, to leave immediately. She ended the session by giving me a long hug. I know that she means well. I know that she cares and I do feel that she wants to help. At first, I felt a little better. She spent over an hour with me talking and praying. It's always nice to be prayed over. But then just like that it was over and I was escorted out of the room and left to figure things out on my own. I have since tried her advice. She told be to say "In the name of Jesus Christ, I rebuke you depression." I try it and sometimes feel more empowered by it. But overall, I'm left wondering what's next? What are my options? Is suicide my only option for relief?

In another note, my Physician told me that she had seen a lady that had constant migraines. She said she could see a black skull cap on this lady's head, except it wasn't a skull cap. It was a demon. They were able to cast it out (I am assuming this was done at her church) and the lady has not had any migraines since. So what should I believe? I still don't know.

It feels like no one wants to see me anymore. I'm a difficult case. After all, the rape occurred some 18 years ago or so. Am I just hanging onto that? Is it me that can't let it go? Is it me that allows the flashbacks, panic attacks, and depression? Is it demons? Can I call the Ghost Busters? Confused and lost is how I feel.

My family has mostly made fun of me since. My brother wants me to put salt around my bed. My mom said she always knew something was wrong with me because of my attitude as a teenager. Very funny people. But really, where does one go from here?

Chapter 16

I saw my therapist, Dolores, today. It was an emotional session for me. I'm just feeling so hopeless, like no one can help me. My psychiatrist doesn't want to see me and my PCP won't change any of my medications. I feel like I lose control just a little more each day.

We got into a deep conversation about fighting back. She asked me what it is that keeps me fighting when I want to give up so badly. So I told her that it feels like I have this little person inside of me that is surrounded by darkness. I imagine her like a mini Wonder Women…in Underoos. Remember those? But hey, at least she has a sword and a shield. My poor little Wonder Woman fighting a losing battle against all this darkness.

Dolores asked me what this person or being needed to keep fighting. I didn't know. I told her she needed to rest and there was only one way to rest. Dolores didn't like that answer as suicide is not an allowable answer. But sometimes it feels as if it is the only answer. As a Game of Thrones connoisseur I imagine my little Wonder Woman being at the bottom of a pile of bodies, like in Battle of the Bastards. She is fighting her way to the top trying to get through the darkness. But the darkness never ends and she is no Jon Snow.

We also talked a lot about my beliefs in God and the afterworld. I had told her about what happened when I visited my PCP and she wanted to know what I had thought about it all. I told her that I had felt rather hopeless following the session as I felt, and still do feel, as if no one can help me. We talked about how believing in God can give someone hope. I explained that I had been trying to use some of the statements my PCP had suggested about revoking the depression or anxiety. There are times when it feels like it is helpful and other times when I want to give up.

I shut down a lot in this session. I do that quite often. When it becomes uncomfortable, I feel like a robot and go into shut down mode. I try to block everything out of my head. I get very tense and I start to cry. Unfortunately, I am usually unable to block things out. Instead, I start focusing on it even more, leaving me crying and feeling out of control and feeling vulnerable, sometimes leading to flashbacks. I hate feeling vulnerable. Vulnerability leads to injury, physical and emotional. But Dolores's office is a safe space for me and I know she won't hurt me. I try so hard to speak but the words won't leave my mouth most of the time.

I know I put her in a difficult position. We can sit there for 15-20 minutes of her trying to reach me and me zoning out. I know she gets frustrated but she never shows it. She just keeps trying. And I feel like it's working, I'm talking to her more and more. Today was a bad day though and she asked me after the session was over to please stay present in the session. Therapy is so hard for me. I think back to all the clients I treated in psychotherapy and I am amazed at the things they were able to share with me. How is it that they can do it but I cannot? What am I doing wrong?

I've been so closed off to my own emotions over the years that it is so hard to open up. If I open up just a little, it all comes flooding out. It has been about 18 years or so since the rape actually happened and about 4 years since the resurgence of my mental illness. How can something that happened over 18 years ago still have so much power over me? How can it still feel like it happens again and again? I saw a video recently of a Veteran. He said, "My war was fought 70 years ago and yesterday." That spoke to me so much. It is exactly what PTSD feels like. I was raped 18 years ago. I had my body torn open and went through so much pain and humiliation. I thought I would be murdered. That was 18 years ago and last night.

So this is what I need to explain to Dolores. This is what she needs to know. It's not anything she is doing. She is amazing. I have to find a way to let her into my head. I feel safe in her office. There's some kind of scent (Apple maybe?) and anytime I smell a similar scent, I think of her and I feel safer. There are a handful of people that I credit for saving my life so far: My mother, my daughter, my best friend Kathleen, and Dolores. I know, that's a lot of pressure to put on other people. But each of these people have given me something when I desperately needed it. Something that makes me think. Something that makes me consider a different alternative. Something that makes me remember that there are reasons for living. Something that makes me choose life each and every day. So thank you to each and every one of you. I can never return what you have given me.

So how does this story end? I wish I could tell you that I am happy, healthy, and symptom free. But what I can tell you is that I am living day by day, sometimes minute by minute. I am here. I matter. I am alive and trying my best to keep it that way.